PIRU SINGH BELONGED TO AN AGRICULTURAL FAMILY OF THE WARRIOR CLAN OF RAJPUTS. HE WAS BORN IN MAY 1918 IN THE VILLAGE OF BERI IN THE JHUNJHUNU DISTRICT OF RAJASTHAN, IN A FAMILY OF 3 BOYS AND 4 GIRLS. HE WAS YOUNGEST OF THE 3 BROTHERS.
AF522516

PIRU WENT TO THE VILLAGE SCHOOL WHEN HE WAS 6 OR 7 YEARS OF AGE. HE, HOWEVER, DID NOT LIKE THE RESTRICTIVE CONDITIONS THERE.

ONE DAY HE HAD A FIGHT WITH A CLASSMATE AND WHEN PUNISHED BY HIS TEACHER, HE GOT ANGRY AND NEVER WENT BACK TO SCHOOL.

INSTEAD OF GOING BACK TO SCHOOL, HE HELPED HIS PARENTS AT THE FARM...

...AND GREW INTO A STRONG, HANDSOME YOUNG MAN.

PIRU WAS FOND OF SPORTS, GAMES AND OUTDOOR LIFE, BUT SHIKAAR WAS HIS FAVOURITE PASTIME AND HE BECAME A GOOD SHOT AT A VERY YOUNG AGE.

At the age of 16, Piru tried to join the army...
Go home son, you are too young.
...but he was rejected twice because he was under age.

Piru was finally accepted when he reached the age of 18 and on 20 May 1935, he joined the army.

Piru was sent to the Punjab regimental centre at Jhelum, which is now part of Pakistan.

After one year of rigorous training...

...Piru was posted to the 5th battalion the Punjab regiment.

Despite his dislike for school in his early years, Piru realized the importance of education and took education in the army seriously.

Within a few years, he passed the army first class certificate of education and was appointed to the rank of Lance Naik on 7 August 1937.

In September 1940 he was posted as an instructor at the Punjab regimental centre at Jhelum. He was promoted to the rank of Naik (corporal) in march 1941...

...and Havildar (sergeant) in February 1942. He saw a lot of action on the North West Frontier during this time.

Piru was an excellent sportsman and represented his regiment in Hockey,...

...Basketball...

...and cross-country.

He was promoted to Company Havildar Major in May 1945 and stayed on the regimental centre till October 1945.

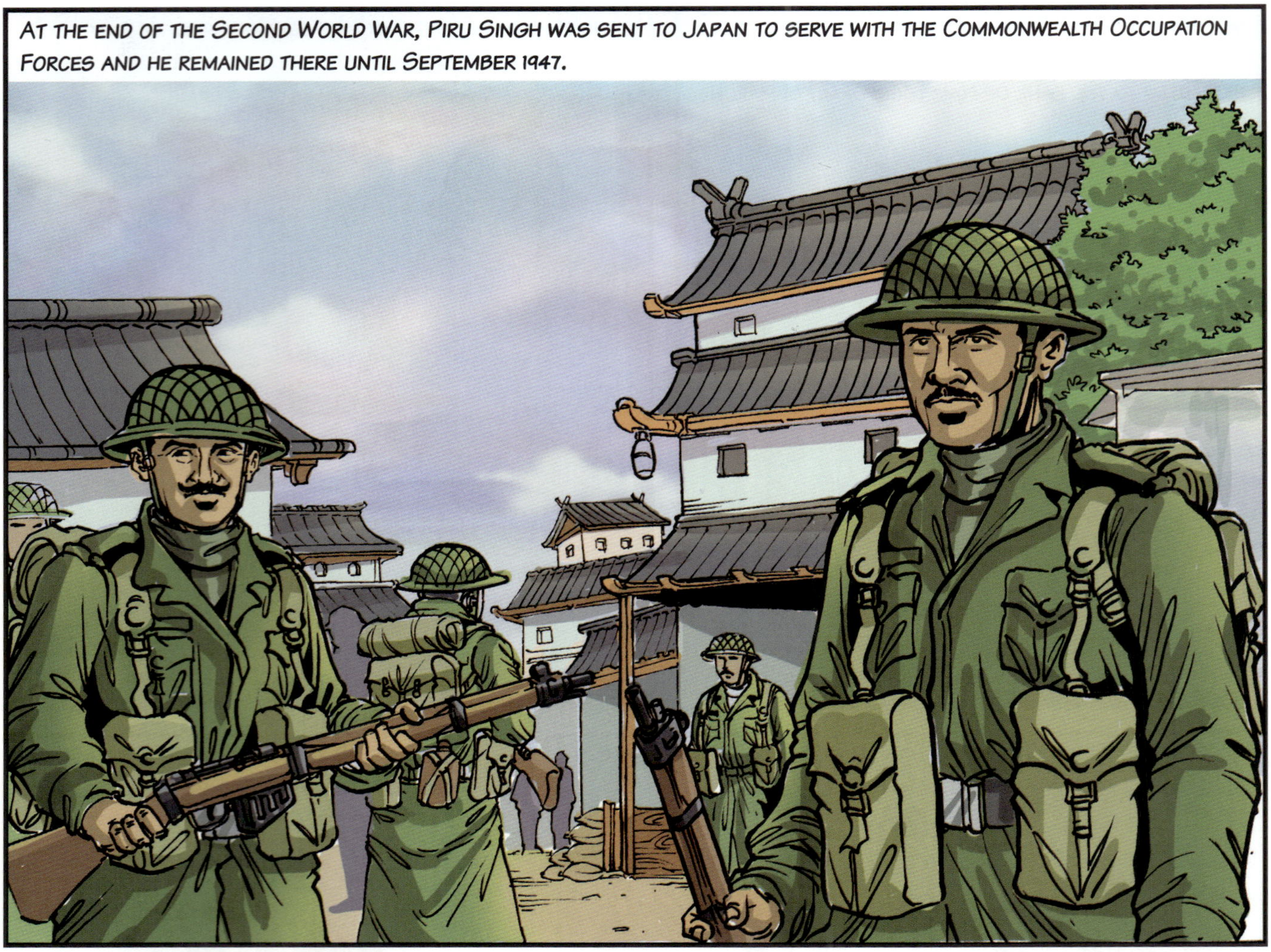

AT THE END OF THE SECOND WORLD WAR, PIRU SINGH WAS SENT TO JAPAN TO SERVE WITH THE COMMONWEALTH OCCUPATION FORCES AND HE REMAINED THERE UNTIL SEPTEMBER 1947.

WHEN THE PARTITION OF THE COUNTRY TOOK PLACE, THE ARMED FORCES WERE ALSO DIVIDED AND THE RAJPUT ELEMENTS OF THE 5TH BATTALION OF THE 1ST PUNJAB REGIMENT WERE TRANSFERRED TO THE 6TH BATTALION THE RAJPUTANA RIFLES.

IDENTICAL TELEGRAMS WERE SENT BY THE PM OF KASHMIR TO DOMINIONS OF INDIA AND PAKISTAN ON 12 AUGUST 1947.
'JAMMU & KASHMIR GOVERNMENT WOULD WELCOME STANDSTILL AGREEMENTS WITH INDIA & PAKISTAN ON ALL MATTERS ON WHICH THESE EXIST AT PRESENT MOMENT WITH OUTGOING BRITISH INDIA GOVERNMENT. IT IS SUGGESTED THAT EXISTING ARRANGEMENTS SHOULD CONTINUE PENDING SETTLEMENT OF DETAILS.'

MEANWHILE, AS IS AUGUST APPROACHED, MAHARAJA HARI SINGH OF J&K ASKED FOR MORE TIME TO MAKE UP HIS MIND, AND ENTERED INTO A 'STANDSTILL AGREEMENT'...

WHEREAS INDIA STOOD BY THE TERMS OF THE AGREEMENT, PAKISTAN WAS IN NO MOOD TO WAIT FOR THE DUE PROCESS OF LAW...

THIS FORCE WAS LED BY OFFICERS...

...JUNIOR COMMISSIONED OFFICERS (JCOs), NON-COMMISSIONED OFFICERS (NCOs) FROM THE REGULAR PAKISTAN ARMY.

THE FORCE WAS SUPPLIED WITH ARMS, AMMUNITION, RATIONS...
GIFTS FROM OUR BRITISH MASTERS!!

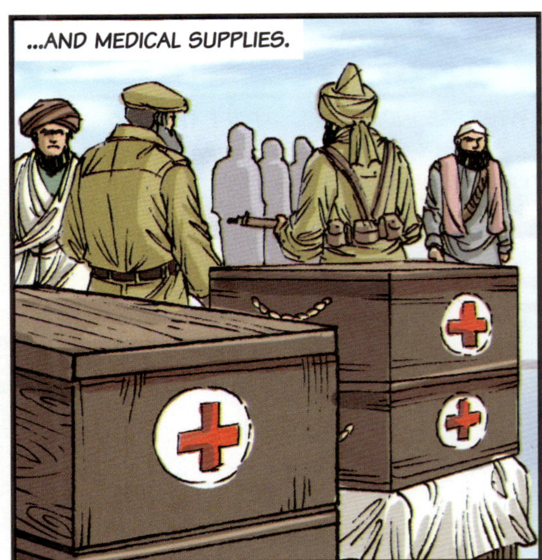
...AND MEDICAL SUPPLIES.

300 CIVILIAN LORRIES WERE HIRED TO TRANSPORT THE FORCE.
LET'S GO MY MUJAHIDS, JIHAD IS NOW. LET'S DESTROY THEM.

ALL THESE ARRANGEMENTS WERE MADE WITH THE FULL SUPPORT AND CONNIVANCE OF THE BRITISH CIVIL & MILITARY AUTHORITIES.

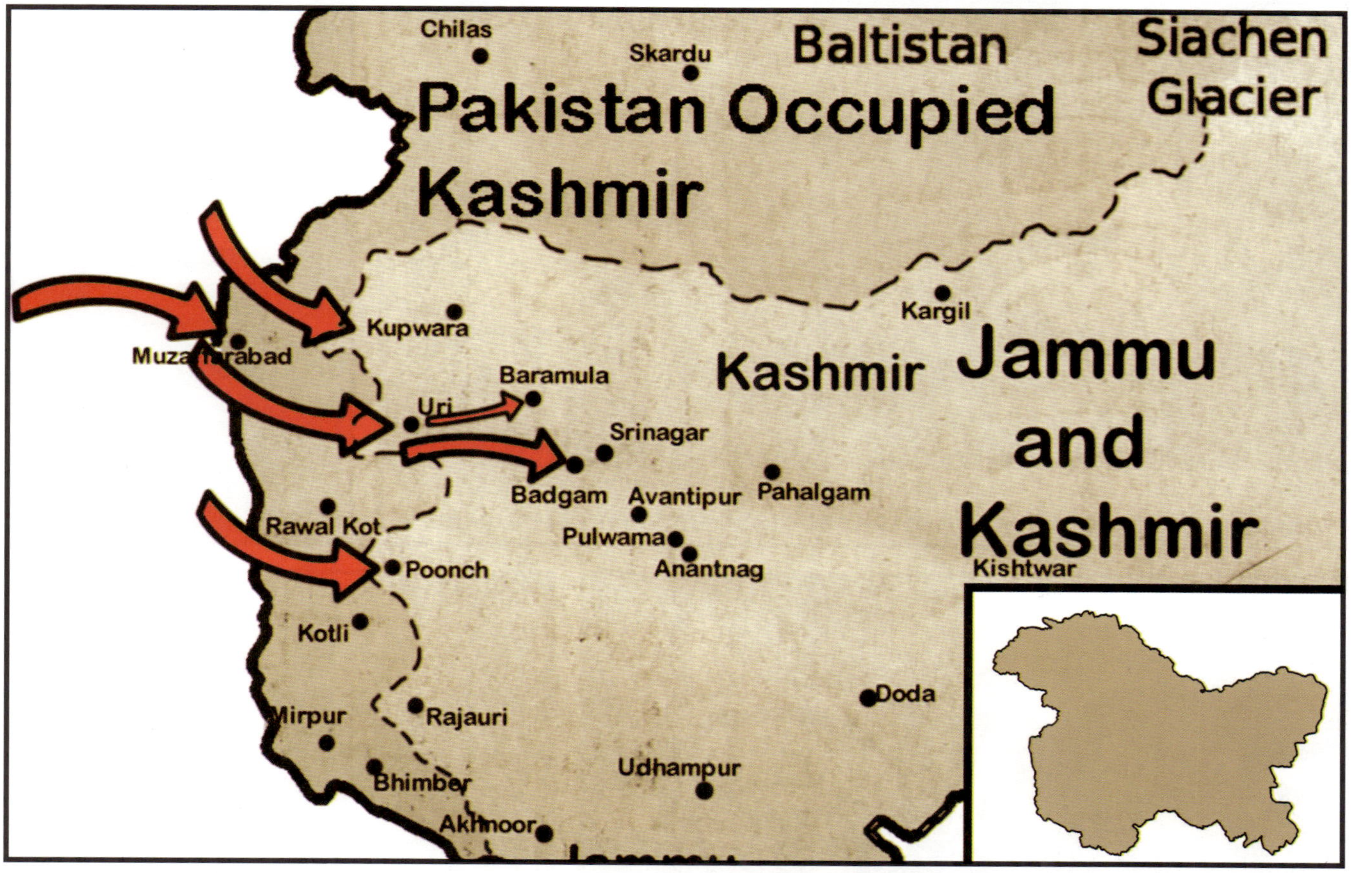

Chilas
Skardu
Baltistan
Siachen Glacier
Pakistan Occupied Kashmir
Kupwara
Muzaffarabad
Kargil
Kashmir
Jammu and Kashmir
Baramula
Uri
Srinagar
Badgam
Avantipur
Pahalgam
Rawal Kot
Pulwama
Poonch
Anantnag
Kishtwar
Kotli
Doda
Mirpur
Rajauri
Bhimber
Udhampur
Akhnoor

*BRIGADIER RAJINDER SINGH IS THE FIRST RECIPIENT OF THE MAHA VIR CHAKRA – INDIA'S SECOND HIGHEST AWARD FOR GALLANTRY IN WAR.

THE CITIES OF DOMEL AND MUZZAFRABAD ALSO FELL.
ALLAH HU AKBAR
ALLAH HU AKBAR

THE MAHARAJA, WHO ALL THIS WHILE WAS VACILLATING WAS UNNERVED AND ON 24 OCTOBER 1947 APPEALED TO THE GOVERNMENT OF INDIA FOR HELP TO REPEL THE INVADERS.
THE GOI INFORMED THE MAHARAJA THAT THEY COULD NOT INTERVENE LAWFULLY WITHOUT THE ACCESSION OF HIS STATE TO THE UNION OF INDIA.

THE MAHARAJA SIGNED THE INSTRUMENT OF ACCESSION ON 26 OCTOBER 1947, WITH THE FULL SUPPORT OF SHEIKH ABDULLAH, THE LEADER OF THE NATIONAL CONFERENCE, THE POLITICAL PARTY WITH THE LARGEST FOLLOWING IN THE STATE...
...AND JAMMU & KASHMIR BECAME AN INTEGRAL PART OF THE UNION OF INDIA – LEGALLY, MORALLY AND CONSTITUTIONALLY.

IT WAS ONLY AFTER THIS THAT THE INDIAN ARMY COMMENCED MAKING PLANS TO EVICT THE RAIDERS, AND 1 SIKH WERE IMMEDIATELY SENT TO SRINAGAR.

WHILE PAKISTAN'S MOVE TO ANNEX JAMMU & KASHMIR BY FORCE WAS A PREMEDITATED PLAN PREPARED SOON AFTER PARTITION WITH THE FULL CONNIVANCE OF THE BRITISH; INDIA HAD MADE NO PLANS FOR MILITARY INTERVENTION IN THE STATE.

ON 26 OCTOBER 1947, THE INDIAN ARMY WAS INFORMED THAT THE STATE OF JAMMU & KASHMIR HAD ACCEDED TO THE UNION OF INDIA.

IT WAS ONLY AFTER THIS THAT THE INDIAN ARMY COMMENCED MAKING A PLAN TO EVICT THE RAIDERS.

MORE INDIAN TROOPS BEGAN TO BE TRANSPORTED TO JAMMU & KASHMIR.

FIRE
SUCCESSFUL BATTLES WERE FOUGHT AT BUDGAM.

AAARGHH
AAARGHH
THE RAIDERS SUFFERED HEAVY LOSSES...

BOOM!!
BOOM!!
...IN THE AND BATTLE OF SHELETANG THE RAIDERS WERE DECISIVELY DEFEATED...

...AFTER WHICH THE THREAT TO SRINAGAR WAS REMOVED.
INDIAN ARMY FORCES CONSOLIDATED GAINS MADE AND CONCENTRATED AT URI.

MAJ GEN K.S. THIMAYYA WAS APPOINTED AS GOC 'SRIDIV' (SRINAGAR DIVISION) TO CONDUCT OPERATIONS IN THE VALLEY.

General Thimayya decided to launch his divisional offensive with the main thrust along the Uri-Domel road with 161 Infantry Brigade under...

...Brigadier L.P. Sen, DSO and 163 Infantry Brigade under...

...Brigadier Harbaksh who was tasked to carry out a diversionary operation towards Tithwal and Handwara to draw away the enemy reserves.

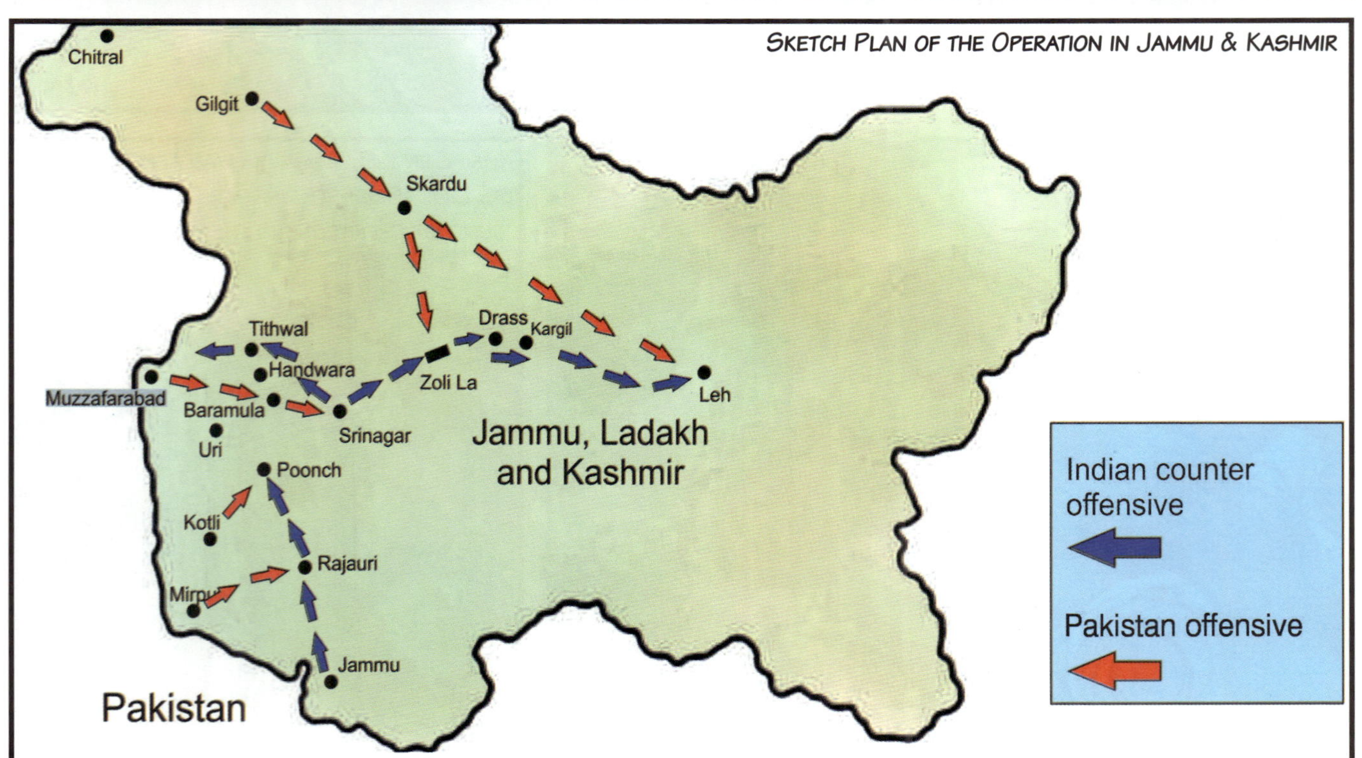
Sketch Plan of the Operation in Jammu & Kashmir
Chitral
Gilgit
Skardu
Tithwal
Handwara
Muzzafarabad
Baramula
Uri
Srinagar
Zoli La
Drass
Kargil
Leh
Poonch
Kotli
Rajauri
Mirpur
Jammu
Pakistan
Jammu, Ladakh and Kashmir
Indian counter offensive
Pakistan offensive

BOTH BRIGADES COMMENCED OPERATIONS IN THE THIRD WEEK OF MAY 1948.

DOGARPUR, TREHGAM AND CHOKIBAL WERE CAPTURED...

...AGAINST STIFF OPPOSITION.

THE ADVANCE TO TITHWAL CONTINUED AND TITHWAL WAS CAPTURED ON 22 MAY 1948.
IT WAS DURING THE TITHWAL OFFENSIVE THAT THE BATTLE OF DARAPARI WAS FOUGHT.

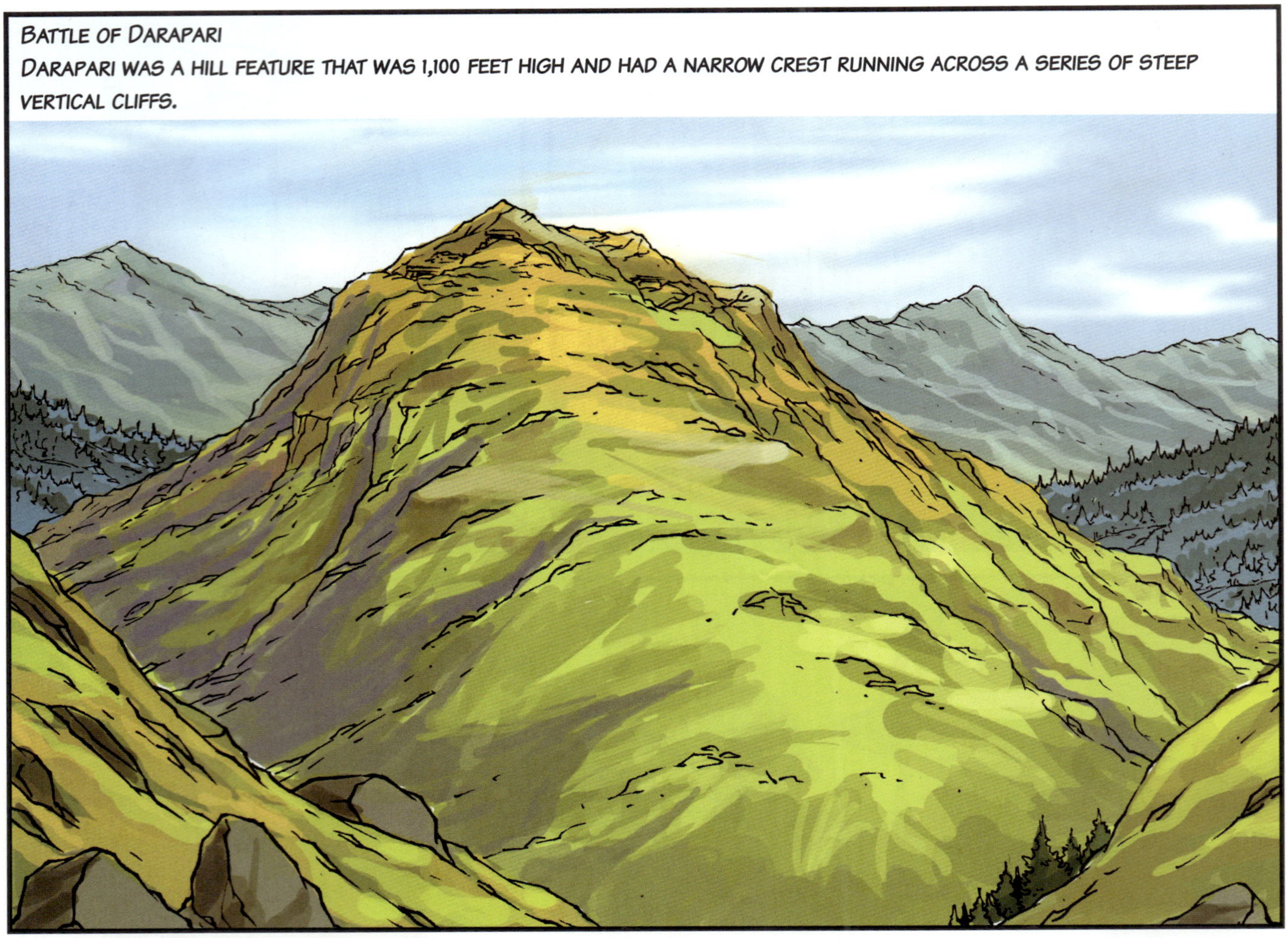

BATTLE OF DARAPARI

DARAPARI WAS A HILL FEATURE THAT WAS 1,100 FEET HIGH AND HAD A NARROW CREST RUNNING ACROSS A SERIES OF STEEP VERTICAL CLIFFS.

6 RAJ RIF (RAJPUTANA RIFLES) WAS TASKED TO CAPTURE THIS FEATURE, WHICH WAS 30 KMS FROM TANGDHAR.

6 RAJ RIF RECEIVED INFORMATION THAT THE PAKISTANIS HAD NOT HAD ENOUGH TIME TO CONSTRUCT STRONG DEFENCES AND COULD THEREFOR BE DISLODGED WITH A QUICK OFFENSIVE.

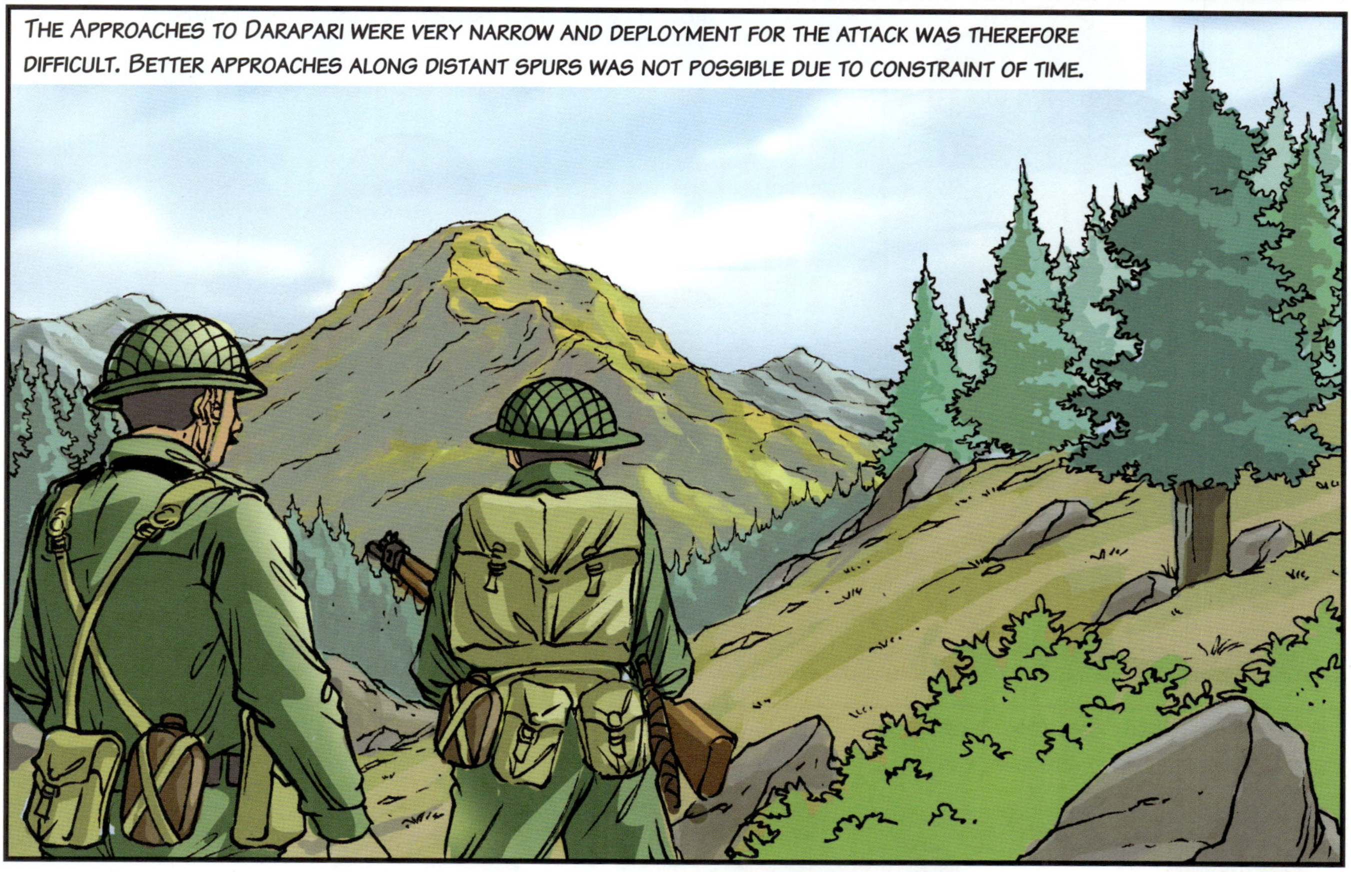

THE APPROACHES TO DARAPARI WERE VERY NARROW AND DEPLOYMENT FOR THE ATTACK WAS THEREFORE DIFFICULT. BETTER APPROACHES ALONG DISTANT SPURS WAS NOT POSSIBLE DUE TO CONSTRAINT OF TIME.

The Darapari hill feature was of vital importance. The Indian Army knew that if Darapari was captured, the whole sector would come under Indian control.
To take advantage of the darkness, the attack for the capture of Darapari was timed for 0130 Hours after the moon had set on the night of 17/18 July.

Troops of 6 Raj Rif headed for the attack on the hill feature.

Prior to the attack, the troops of Raj Rif began to formulate their attack plan.

It is going to be a tough nut to crack, but we have to do it!!

THE ENEMY HAD VERY STRONG POSITIONS AND THEY HAD SITED THEIR MEDIUM MACHINE GUNS (MMGS) TO COVER ALL POSSIBLE APPROACHES...

...THIS, ALONG WITH THE PROBLEM OF VERY NARROW APPROACHES MADE THE TASK FOR 6 RAJ RIF VERY DIFFICULT.

THE INDIANS WILL BE LAUNCHING THEIR ATTACK, I HOPE ALL THE DEFENCES ARE STRENGTHENED.
YES, WE ARE READY, LET THEM COME!..

ELSEWHERE AT THE INDIAN POSITION...
BEFORE WE LAUNCH THE ATTACK WE MOVE TO THE FORWARD LOCATIONS.

LET'S MOVE OUT!!!

The defending Pakistanis fired a flare in anticipation of an attack.

Damn it, they have launched flares!
We are sure to be spotted!!

Indians are attacking!!!
Death to the infidels, Allah hu Akbar!!!

Kill them!
RAT-TAT-TAT-TAT
TAT TAT TAT

Death to you!
BOOM!!

When 'D' company, 6 Raj Rif reached close to the enemy defences, all hell broke loose from all sides.
AAARGHH
RAT-TAT-TAT-TAT
TAT TAT TAT

BOOOOOM!!
KEEP FIRING! KEEP MOVING!...
AS THE ATTACK ADVANCED, IT WAS MET WITH HEAVY MACHINE GUN FIRE FROM BOTH FLANKS.

DESPITE ENEMY FIRE PIRU SINGH ADVANCED...
RAT-TAT-TAT-TAT TAT TAT TAT

TAKE THIS, YOU INFIDELS...!!

...AGAINST VOLLEYS OF GRENADES BEING HURLED DOWN FROM THE ENEMY BUNKERS.
BOOOOOM!!
AAARGHH
AAARGHH

ONE OF THE SOLDIERS, BHIKA SINGH CHARGED AT THE ENEMY WITH GUNS BLAZING.
LET'S GET THEM MEN!

AAARGHH
AAARGHH

SUBEDAR BHIKA SINGH THE PLATOON COMMANDER WAS HIT BY A BULLET.
BOOOOM!!
AAARGHH

SEEING THAT THE PLATOON COMMANDER WAS GRIEVOUSLY WOUNDED, PIRU SINGH TOOK COMMAND AND LED THIS GALLANT PLATOON AGAINST THE MURDEROUS FIRE...

...COMING FROM THE PAKISTANIS DEPLOYED IN WELL-DUG TRENCHES AND BUNKERS LOCATED ON HIGH GROUND.

PIRU THEN TOOK COMMAND AND LED HIS GALLANT PLATOON

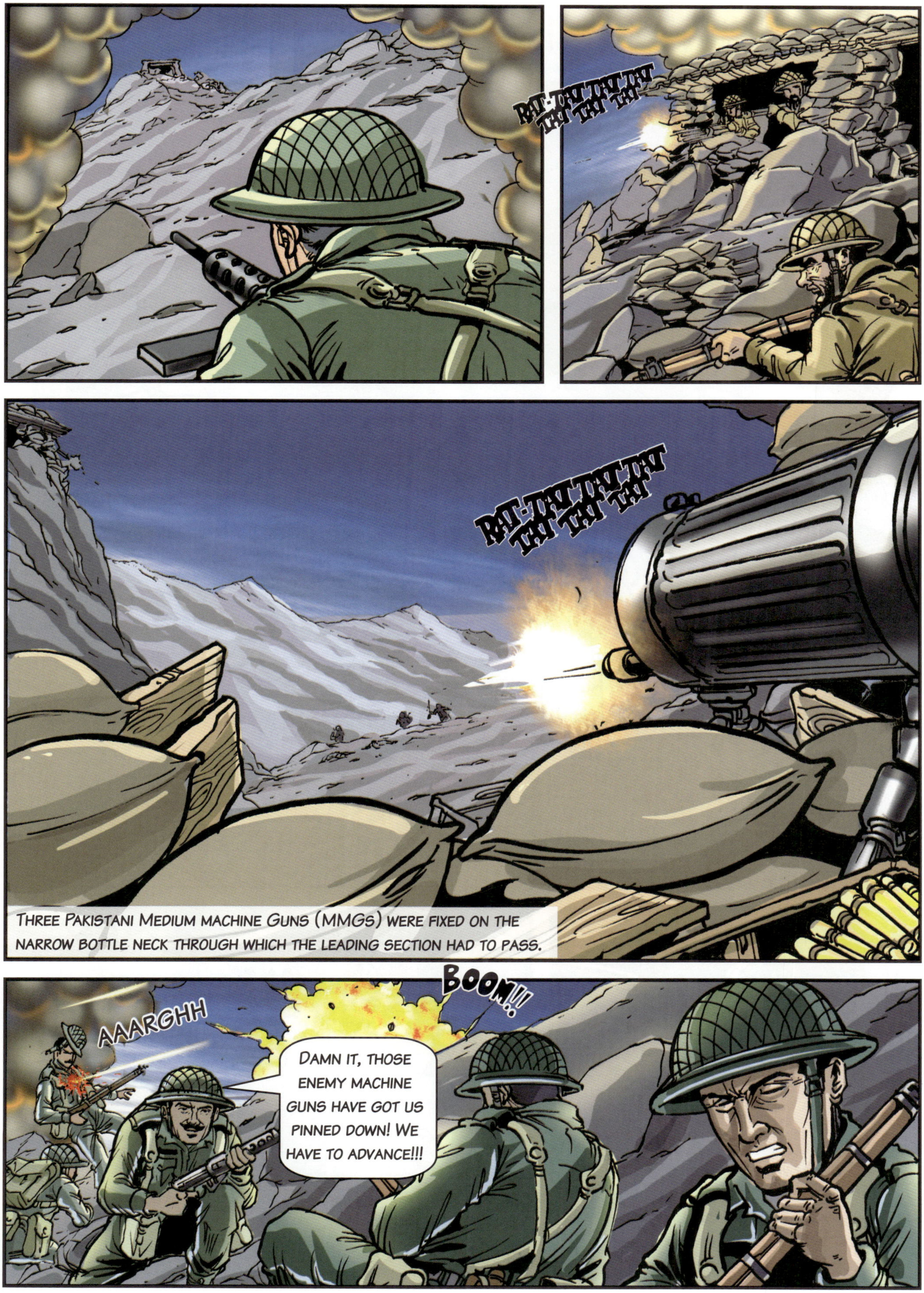

THREE PAKISTANI MEDIUM MACHINE GUNS (MMGS) WERE FIXED ON THE NARROW BOTTLE NECK THROUGH WHICH THE LEADING SECTION HAD TO PASS.

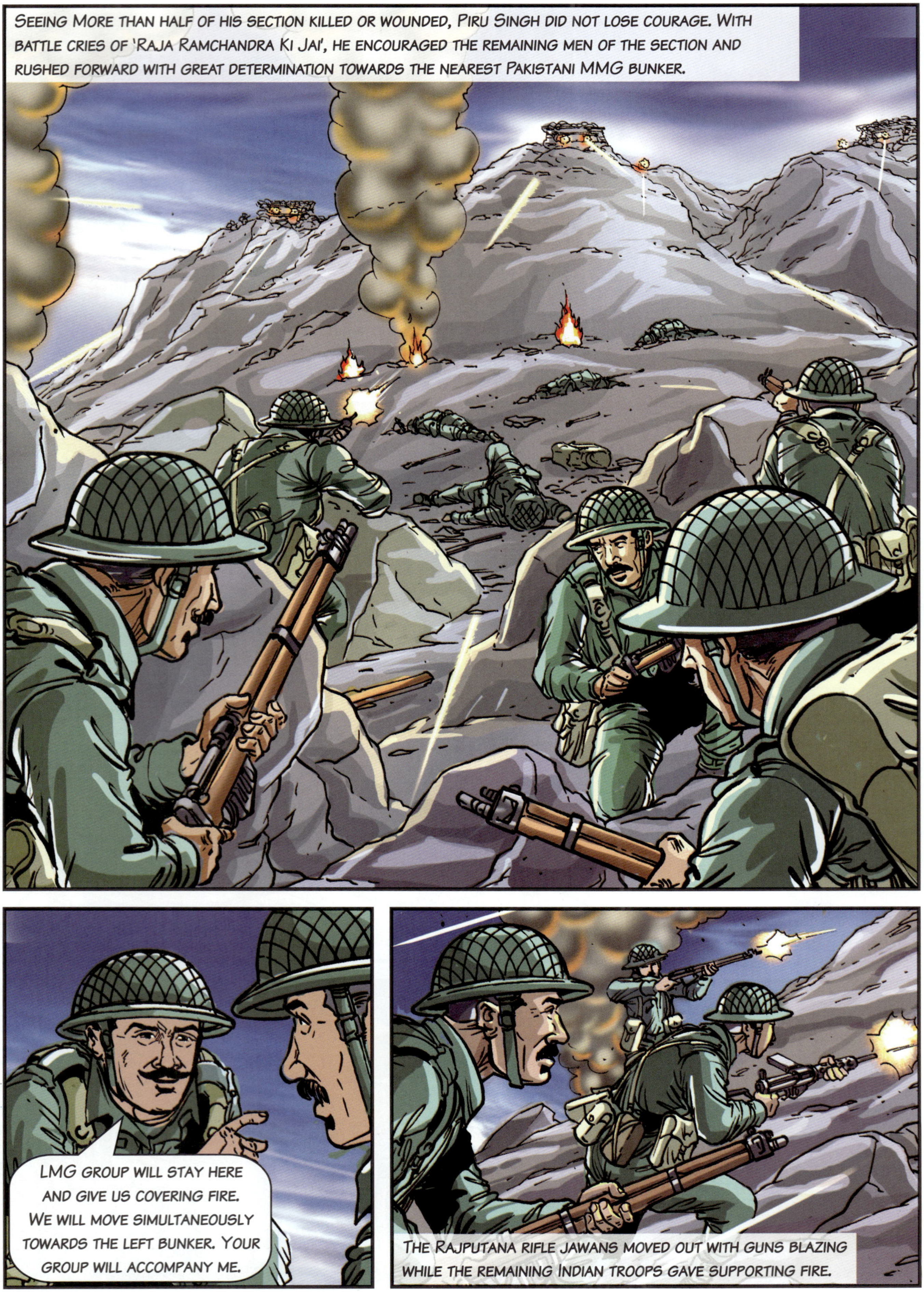

Seeing More than half of his section killed or wounded, Piru Singh did not lose courage. With battle cries of 'Raja Ramchandra Ki Jai', he encouraged the remaining men of the section and rushed forward with great determination towards the nearest Pakistani MMG bunker.

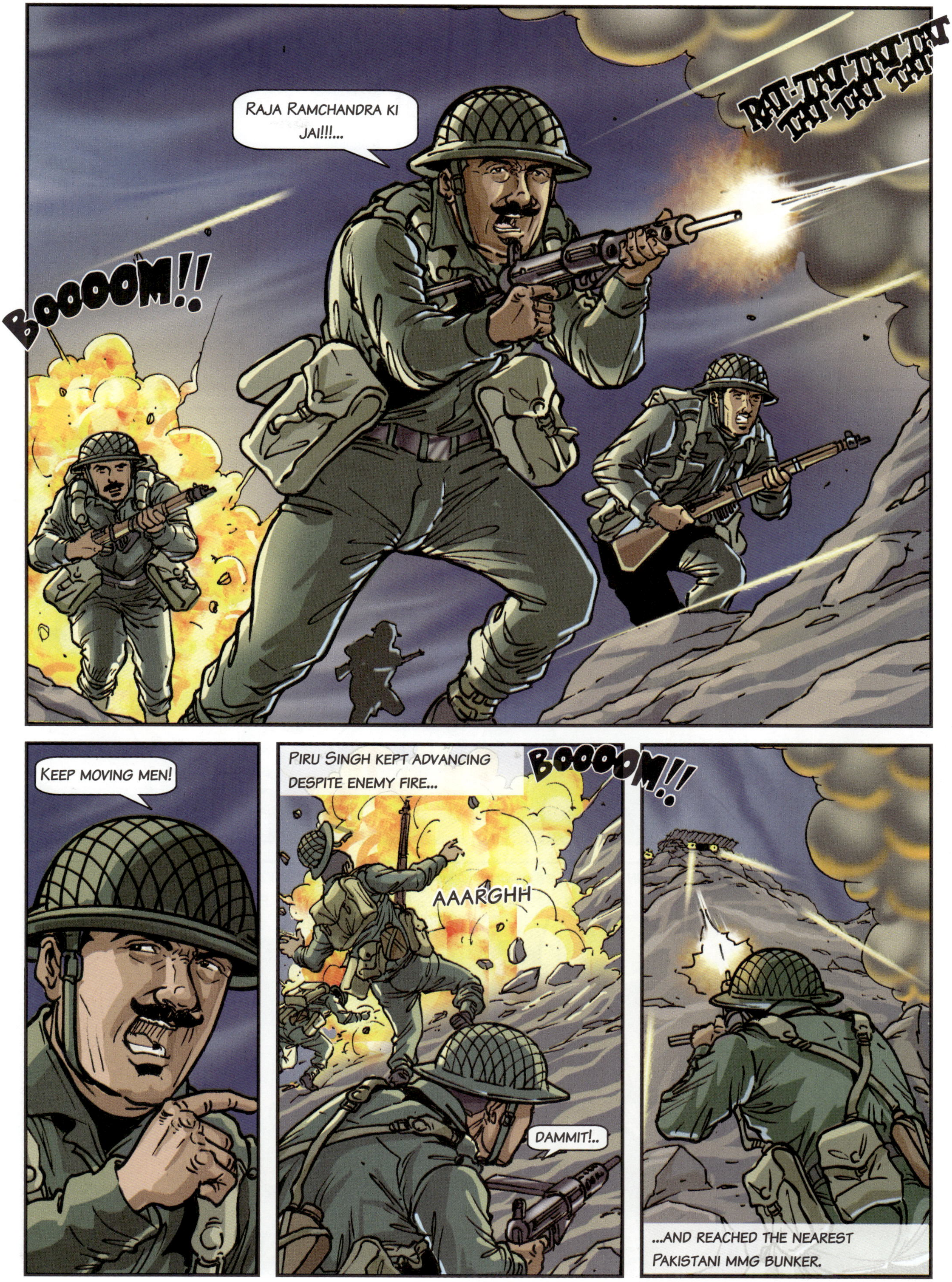

Raja Ramchandra ki jai!!!...
RAT-TAT TAT TAT
TAT TAT TAT
BOOOOM!!

WITHOUT REGARD FOR HIS PERSONAL SAFETY HE ADVANCED TOWARDS A PAKISTANI MMG BUNKER BLAZING AT THE OCCUPANTS THUS SILENCING THE ENEMY MEDIUM MACHINE GUN.
AAARGHH
PIRU SINGH CHARGED AMIDST ENEMY BULLETS AND BOMBS.

KAFIRS OVER THERE, KILL THEM!

BOOOOM!!
AAARGHH
BOOOOM!!
A GRENADE EXPLODED NEAR HIM.

THE GRENADE SPLINTERS RIPPED THROUGH HIS CLOTHES WOUNDING HIM IN SEVERAL PLACES BUT HE DECIDED TO CONTINUE TO ADVANCE.

THE INDIAN TROOPS KEPT UP WITH THEIR FIRE TARGETING THE ENEMY POSITIONS. THUS DRAWING THEIR ATTENTION.

PIRU SINGH MANAGED TO REACH NEAR THE BUNKER.
I AM VERY CLOSE TO THE ENEMY!

TAKE THIS GRENADE YOU @#$#

BOOOOM!!
AAARGHH

THE INDIAN TROOPS KEPT CONTINUOUSLY DRAWING ENEMY ATTENTION SO AS TO SUPPORT PIRU SINGH IN HIS ATTACK.
I SEE MORE KAFIRS OVER THERE... KILL THEM!!
RAT-TAT-TAT-TAT TAT-TAT-TAT

THE ENEMY FAILED TO NOTICE THAT PIRU SINGH HAD MANAGED TO CREEP UNOBSERVED ALONG THEIR FLANK.

WITHOUT REGARD FOR HIS PERSONAL SAFETY, HE ADVANCED TOWARDS A PAKISTANI MMG BUNKER.

THE ENEMY SOLDIERS WERE TAKEN BY SURPRISE.
AAARGHH

AAARGH
AAARGH
HE BLAZED AWAY AT THE OCCUPANTS THUS SILENCING THE ENEMY MEDIUM MACHINE GUN.

GNNHH!!

BY THEN PIRU SINGH REALIZED THAT HE WAS THE SOLE SURVIVOR OF THE SECTION, THE REST BEING EITHER KILLED OR WOUNDED.
SO MANY OF MY BROTHERS HAVE SACRIFICED THEIR LIVES.

I WILL AVENGE THEM!!!

BOOOOOM!!
PIRU HEADED TOWARDS THE NEXT ENEMY BUNKER.

BOOM!!
WHAT THE!? OUR MACHINE GUN POST HAS BEEN DESTROYED?? BUT HOW!?
THAT MEANS THE KAFIRS MUST HAVE BREACHED OUR FLANKS.

I SEE AN INDIAN SOLDIER HEADING THIS WAY. LET ME DEAL WITH HIM!

ANOTHER GRENADE WAS THROWN AT HIM...
TAKE THIS, YOU @#$#

...WOUNDING PIRU SINGH.
BOOOOOM!!
AAARGHH

WITH BLOOD DRIPPING FROM HIS FACE, PIRU SINGH HURLED GRENADES AT THE NEXT ENEMY POSITION.

BOOOOM!!
AAARGHH
EEAARGH!

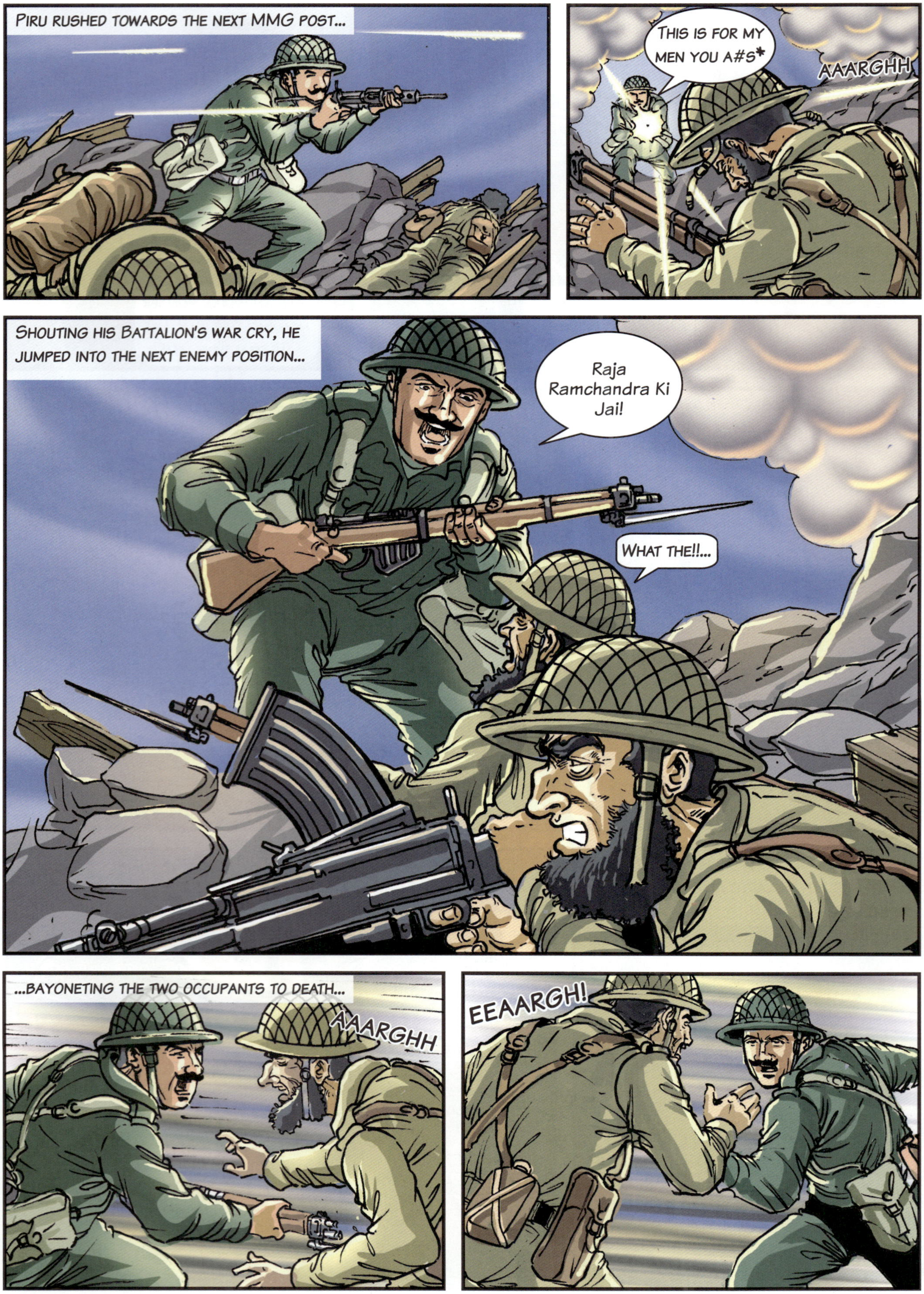

SHOUTING HIS BATTALION'S WAR CRY, HE JUMPED INTO THE NEXT ENEMY POSITION...

Raja Ramchandra Ki Jai!

WHAT THE!!...

AS PIRU SINGH EMERGED FROM THE SECOND TRENCH
THERE IS STILL ONE MORE MACHINE GUN POST REMAINING, MUST DEAL WITH!...

A KAFIR SOLDIER OVER THERE!...
KILL HIM!!...

THAT'S THE LAST BUNKER; MUST DESTROY IT...
RAT-TAT-TAT-TAT
TAT TAT TAT
HE CHARGED AT THE THIRD ENEMY TRENCH

PIRU SINGH'S GUN JAMMED
DAMN IT, NOT NOW! I AM SO CLOSE TO THE ENEMY POSITION

I HAVE ONLY THIS GRENADE!! MUST MAKE IT COUNT!

MUST GET CLOSE TO THEM!

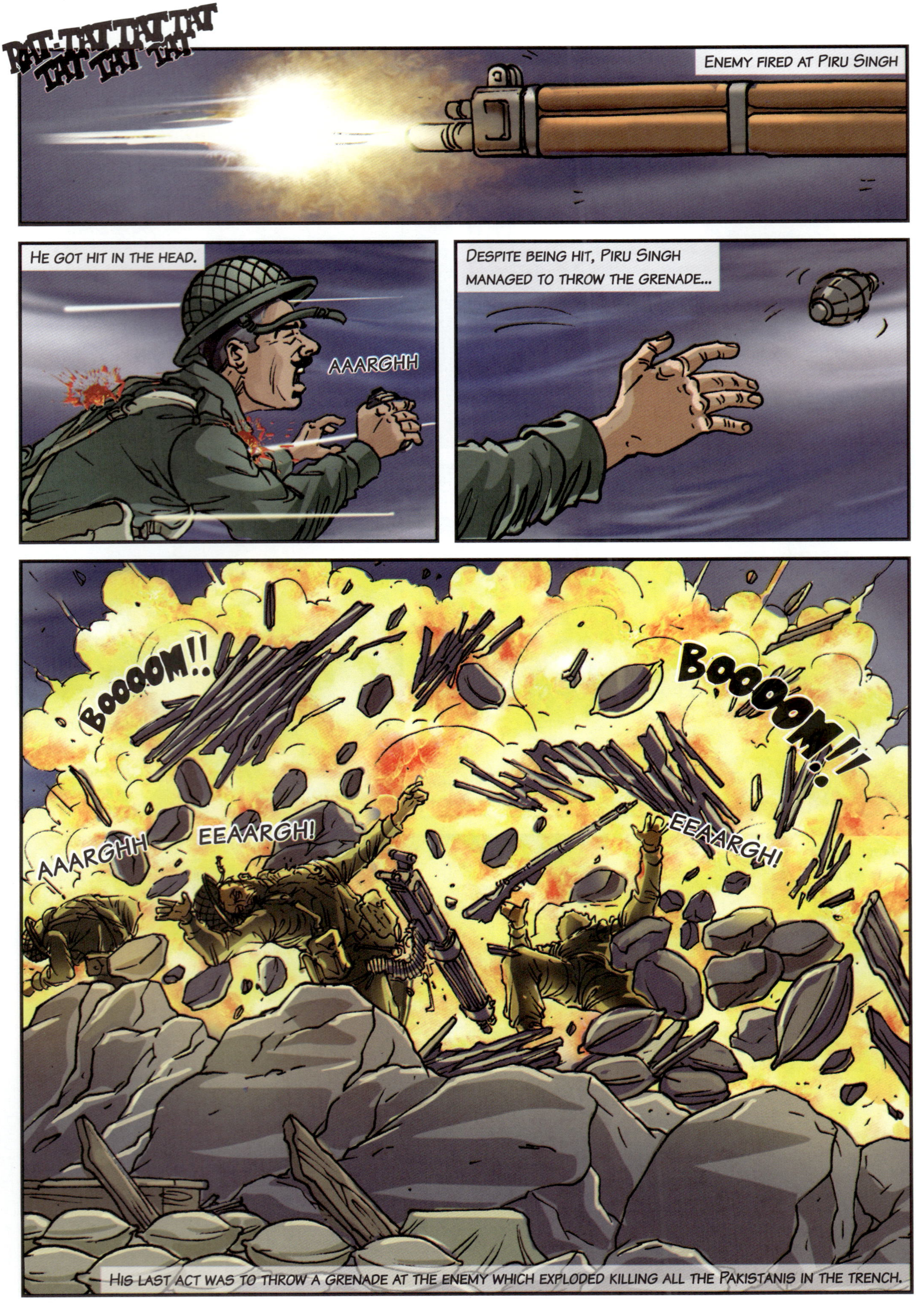

BOOOOM!!

BOOOOM!!

AAARGHH

EEAARGH!

EEAARGH!

His last act was to throw a grenade at the enemy which exploded killing all the Pakistanis in the trench.

PIRU SINGH PAID WITH HIS LIFE FOR HIS SINGULARLY BRAVE ACT BUT HE LEFT THE INDIAN ARMY WITH A UNIQUE EXAMPLE OF SINGLE-HANDED BRAVERY AND DETERMINED COLD COURAGE.
BHARAT MATA KI JAI
COMPANY HAVILDAR MAJOR PIRU SINGH PLAYED A SIGNIFICANT ROLE IN THE SUCCESS OF HIS BATTALION'S CAPTURE OF THE PAKISTANI DEFENSIVE POSITION AT DARAPARI...

...WHICH IN TURN HELPED IN PUSHING THE RAIDERS BEYOND URI.
IN ADDITION TO THE PART PLAYED BY 6 RAJ RIF IN THE CAPTURE OF PIRKANTI AND LEDIGALLI...

...THE COURAGE DISPLAYED BY PIRU SINGH IN THE CAPTURE OF DARAPARI FURTHER ENHANCED THE REPUTATION OF 6 RAJ RIF.

MESSAGE FROM PIRU SINGH'S LIFE FOR THE CITIZENS OF INDIA

'EVERYONE IS AFRAID OF SOMETHING. COURAGE MEANS OVERCOMING FEAR. BE BRAVE AND FACE ALL OBSTACLES IN YOUR LIFE WITH COURAGE AND YOU WILL HAVE A MEANINGFUL LIFE.'

PIRU SINGH'S OUTSTANDING LEADERSHIP AND COLD COURAGE DEMONSTRATED AT THE BATTLE OF DARAPARI WAS AN OUTSTANDING EXAMPLE OF PERSONAL LEADERSHIP WHICH MERITED INDIA'S HIGHEST AWARD FOR COURAGE IN THE FACE OF THE ENEMY. PIRU SINGH LOST HIS LIFE, BUT HIS ACTS OF COURAGE ARE ETERNAL.